# the appraisal
# discussion

TERRY GILLEN

**Terry Gillen** is a Fellow of the IPD and Member of the Institute of Management. His career in training began over 20 years ago, taking him from the public sector, through the private sector and into consultancy. As well as working with clients independently, he tutors for Ashridge Management College, Jersey's Highlands College Management Development Centre, CareerTrack International, and the IPD. He is a regular contributor to *People Management*. His books include *Positive Influencing Skills* (1995), *Assertiveness* Adair's Management Development Exercis

**Management Shapers** is a comprehensive series covering all the crucial management skill areas. Each book includes the key issues, helpful starting points and practical advice in a concise and lively style. Together, they form an accessible library reflecting current best practice – ideal for study or quick reference.

## Other titles in the series:

*Constructive Feedback*
Roland and Frances Bee

*The Disciplinary Interview*
Alan Fowler

*Listening Skills* (Second edition)
Ian MacKay

*Negotiating, Persuading and Influencing*
Alan Fowler

*The Selection Interview*
Penny Hackett

The Institute of Personnel and Development is the leading publisher of books and reports for personnel and training professionals, students, and all those concerned with the effective management and development of people at work. For full details of all our titles please contact the Publishing Department:
*tel.* 0181-263 3387
*fax* 0181-263 3850
*e-mail* publish@ipd.co.uk
The catalogue of all IPD titles can be viewed on the IPD website:
http://www.ipd.co.uk

# the**appraisal discussion**

TERRY GILLEN

INSTITUTE OF PERSONNEL AND DEVELOPMENT

First published in the *Training Extras* series in 1995
Reprinted 1996, 1997
First published in the *Management Shapers* series in 1998

Typesetting by Paperweight
Printed in Great Britain by
The Guernsey Press, Channel Islands

*British Library Cataloguing in Publication Data*
A catalogue record for this book is available from the
British Library

ISBN
0-85292-751-7

INSTITUTE OF PERSONNEL
AND DEVELOPMENT

IPD House, Camp Road, London SW19 4UX
Tel.: 0181 971 9000   Fax: 0181 263 3333
Registered office as above. Registered Charity No. 1038333.
A company limited by guarantee. Registered in England No. 2931892.

# contents

# appraisal

Organisations employ a wide range of appraisal systems. Some are very manager-led, where the appraiser writes the documentation and shares it with the appraisee. In others, the appraiser's role is to help the appraisee evaluate their contribution to organisational performance. In some organisations, appraisals are dominated by the remuneration implications of performance ratings. In others, salary reviews, performance reviews, and career reviews are all separate. Whatever your appraisal experience, there will be one constant – the effectiveness of the appraisal discussion determines the effectiveness of the whole appraisal system. It also affects the appraiser's credibility as a manager and the performance of the appraiser's staff.

## The changing face of appraisal

Formal appraisal has its roots in large bureaucratic organisations where it was normal to tell staff how they were performing, what training they would get, into which jobs they would be transferred, and to what level they would be promoted. The annual appraisal was the means by which the relevant information was gained.

As administrators of the process, custodians of the information, and the prime users of information related to training needs and succession planning, personnel departments were usually seen as the 'owners' of the appraisal system. Line managers, by inference, performed the annual ritual on personnel's behalf.

The 1980s and 1990s have seen growing emphasis on performance, and hence on performance reviews. In the UK, at least, this impetus continued with the focus on performance caused by successive economic recessions, the application of commercial philosophies to the public sector, and with the widening adoption of PRP (performance-related pay).

Opinions on the values of appraisal schemes vary. While few people would want to do away with such a prime opportunity to foster discussion between managers and their staff or to gather valuable data, traditional appraisal, where the appraisee is a passive recipient of the appraiser's opinions, seems increasingly 'past its sell-by date' in the current environment. It makes sense, therefore, to consider exactly why we want appraisal.

## The purpose of appraisal

Appraisal, where it is done positively, has many benefits and many beneficiaries, illustrated on page 3. You may well be able to think of numerous other benefits, but the overriding advantage of appraisal is that performance should improve – and that benefits everyone. This, then, is the main reason

## *Appraisal benefits and beneficiaries*

**Organisation**
- ○ Data on organisational performance.
- ▣ HR planning data.
- ▲ Better communication.
- ○ Better motivation.
- ○ Better organisational performance.

**Appraisee**
- ○ Better understanding of performance requirements, leading to better performance.
- ▣ Opportunity to discuss problems and grievances.
- ▲ Focus on you and your needs.

**Appraiser**
- ○ Better staff performance.
- ▣ Problem rectification.
- ▲ Feedback on self.

for appraisal: *quality feedback improves performance.* That is central to modern management.

## The purpose of management

Management is there to connect employees to the results that need to be achieved if the organisation is to achieve its purpose. In today's environment, that requires motivation. Motivation is a complex issue, but for the vast majority of people there are certain constants: we perform better when we feel good about what we do and that good feeling is fostered through recognition, praise, positive feedback of results, good working relationships, and so on. Motivation is also necessary for continual learning. Together they are, I believe, essential to peak performance. By encouraging motivation and facilitating learning, everyone can improve. The simplest route for managers to follow, therefore, in connecting people to results is to:

- set challenging goals
- monitor and give positive feedback of performance
- ▲ identify ways their staff can improve their value in their current jobs and, over the longer term, to the organisation as a whole.

That is not only effective management, it is effective appraisal.

## Overview of content

To help you appraise effectively, this book:

- describes the problems people typically encounter in appraisal
- shows you how to prepare for and lead an appraisal discussion so that you not only avoid the problems but so that you, and everyone else, gain maximum benefit from the process.

This content is based on my experience of designing and running appraisal-skills programmes over many years. During that time I have listened to appraisers and appraisees to find out their concerns and frustrations with appraisal, the problems they encounter, and what they want out of it. I have also listened to the views of senior line managers and personnel specialists. Wittingly and unwittingly, they have contributed to what I hope is the practical nature of this book. It is not meant to be a comprehensive treatise on appraisal[1]. It approaches the subject unashamedly from the viewpoint of appraisers on the basis that:

- organisations demand a lot of appraisers, and too frequently send them into the fray with too little training – they genuinely need help

- appraisal has the potential to soak up a tremendous amount of managers' time. The ideal, therefore, is for appraisers to use their time wisely while generating maximum benefit from the appraisal process. Hence this book is intended to be practical, helpful, and quick and easy to read.

**Note**: I refer to two types of appraisal: *formal* appraisal, which is still usually an annual affair conducted as part of the organisation's policy, and *routine* or *informal* appraisal, which is carried out more frequently as a matter between managers and their staff. Also, I use the term 'manager' to describe anyone who has responsibility for people who report to them, so it includes chief executives, junior team-leaders, and everyone in between.

## End-note

[1] In my opinion, the best book in that category is *Appraisal* by Clive Fletcher, published by the IPD, second edition 1997.

# preparation

Think of the problems you can encounter in appraisal; there are three root problems.

**Perceptions of appraisal**. Where people see appraisal as an administrative chore, they are likely to devote insufficient time and attention to it and so experience disadvantages such as disagreements, strained relationships, and so on.

**Standing in judgement**. To one extent or another appraisal involves an appraiser giving an appraisee feedback on their performance. In some schemes this is summarised on an alphanumeric scale relating to an appraisee's overall performance for the year. For example:

Performance rating 1 = Outstanding performance; significantly exceeds job requirements.

Performance rating 2 = Very good performance; exceeds job requirements.

Performance rating 3 = Satisfactory performance; meets job requirements.

Performance rating 4    =    Unsatisfactory; does not meet job requirements.

Performance rating 5    =    Very unsatisfactory; significantly fails to meet job requirements.

While in a minority of schemes the feedback is given with a coaching-style dialogue, during which appraisers help appraisees evaluate their own performance, most of the time it involves one person 'standing in judgement' on another. This 'judgement' ingredient to appraisal often encourages the two parties inadvertently to polarise their approaches. Appraisees approach appraisal from a defensive position. Appraisers, on the other hand, tend to look for 'improvement areas', which makes it easy for them to be critical.

**Lack of involvement, leading to lack of ownership.** Many appraisers allow appraisees to be too passive in the appraisal process – the *whole* process. The result is that appraisees are 'on the receiving end' and that gives rise to surprises, polarisation of views, and difficulties where none need exist.

These problems can be avoided with proper preparation. While most things in life are easier if we prepare for them, in appraisal it is doubly important. First, because without it appraisal can never be as effective as it could be and, second, virtually all the preparation is, itself, beneficial management practice. So in this section I am going to show you how to prepare for appraisal as easily and as effectively as possible by taking the following six steps. They begin broadly, with you and your attitude, and gradually become more and more specific until you are preparing the logistics for an individual discussion.

## Step 1 – Prepare your mind

Check the mind-set with which you approach appraisals. Do you think of appraisal conversations as interviews or as discussions? If you think of them as interviews, you probably still regard appraisal (and hence improved performance) as something that managers *do* to their staff rather than as something they work on *with* them. Thinking of them as discussions between two equal parties is much more positive. (While you may not be 'equals' as far as the organisation structure is concerned, you both share a common interest in achieving a worthwhile outcome from the discussion. That is achieved more easily if you approach the discussion as equals.)

You both have rights in that discussion. The table on page 10 contains a selection of rights by way of illustration.

Central to these rights are honesty and accuracy in giving feedback, and a willingness to listen to each other. That only happens when appraiser and appraisee feel they are equal parties to the discussion.

Also remember that, as an appraiser, you may have numerous appraisals to complete as well as your other duties. From each

## *Appraisers' and appraisees' rights*

| Appraiser's rights | Appraisee's rights |
|---|---|
| ⊙ to give honest and accurate feedback | ⊙ to be given sufficient preparation time |
| ▣ to control the overall pace and direction of the discussion | ▣ to have an appraiser who owns up to his or her mistakes |
| △ to criticise constructively, reprimand or discipline appraisee, where appropriate | △ to receive fair and consistent treatment |
| ⊙ to be listened to and have views considered | ⊙ to respond to criticism |
| ⊙ to disagree with appraisee | ⊙ to receive reasons and explanations for appraiser's opinions |
| ⊙ to expect honesty from appraisee | ⊙ to criticise the appraiser |
| ▣ to give instructions to, and make requests of, appraisee | ▣ to be listened to |
| △ to receive co-operation from appraisee | △ to expect honesty from appraiser |
| ⊙ not to be 'blackmailed' by appraisee's reaction to criticism | ⊙ to choose not to answer personal or unreasonable questions |
| | ⊙ to feel OK about the discussion |

appraisee's viewpoint, however, it looks very different. It is their opportunity, sometimes only an annual opportunity, to have your undivided attention discussing nothing other than them, their job, and their future.

## Step 2 – Understand the job

Recommending that you understand the job of the appraisee you are about to appraise may sound a bit odd to many appraisers, but consider the following points:

● No one understands a job like the person actually doing it; so unless you are the person processing the documents, keying-in the data, repairing the machines, satisfying the customers, making the decisions, or agreeing the loans, it is safe to assume that your understanding of the job is not as thorough as theirs.

■ You may have done the job yourself, but the speed of change in most organisations, the effects of downsizing, rationalisation, and new technology mean that experiences can quickly become out-of-date.

▲ Appraisees often spend more time with people (customers, suppliers, colleagues, managers of other departments) other than their appraisers.

In short, it is not possible to appraise someone's performance without a good understanding of their job, and in today's environment, that understanding is worth refreshing. An effective way of doing that is to consider the job's purpose and key result areas.

**Job purpose**. Thinking through the purpose of the job in terms which are both concise and incisive is a major help to you, by providing an 'acid test' for most aspects of performance. Here are some examples. The maintenance engineering manager, whose official job purpose is to provide an efficient and effective maintenance engineering service is really there to keep the plant running. The computer repair person whose official job purpose is to respond to requests for assistance from customers within designated time frames and to effect repairs within budget whilst achieving high rates of customer satisfaction is really there to make customers glad we service their equipment. The librarian who runs a stodgy old library in a company about to be revitalised as it seeks out new markets might have an official job purpose to manage the library within agreed budgets, providing a timely information service to departments but is really there to transform the old-fashioned library into a business-led information resource-centre.

This kind of precision will help you understand the job, identify the essential elements of good performance, and review the actual performance of the job-holder. It also helps appraisees. It is like having their own personal and illuminating mission statement. Not many statements of job purpose are that concise, which is why, when you ask people what they are employed for, most of them tell you what they are called ('I'm a customer services assistant') or they tell you what they do ('I process order forms'). They do not tell you why their job exists.

**Key result areas**. Once you have specified the job purpose, it becomes easier to identify the five or six areas in which results must be achieved if the job purpose is to be fulfilled. They are the key result areas.

Our maintenance engineering manager, for example, might have KRAs for maintenance schedules, response times, staff, budgets and future development. Our computer repair person might have KRAs for response times, customer satisfaction, cost control, technical knowledge and image. Our company librarian might have KRAs for stock, customer satisfaction, budgets, staff and future development. This approach to understanding a job has three main benefits. First, areas such as image, response times and staff, if they are key to fulfilment of the job purpose, are included rather than being all-too-easily overlooked. Second, being the first part of an approach to objective setting, it results in objectives which are 100 per cent relevant to the job and which include all relevant areas. Third, it makes it easy to assess current performance.

## Step 3 – Assess current performance

Assessing current performance is central to appraisal. It is from this assessment that performance ratings (if your scheme has them), training needs, future objectives, and possibly even future career, can stem. Your ability accurately to assess performance, and communicate that assessment, will also affect the outcome of the appraisal discussion and your credibility in the eyes of the appraisee, so it makes sense to get it right. An important aspect of getting it right is the ability (and willingness) to avoid bias.

## Avoiding bias

Bias is a bit like the proverbial iceberg in that much of it is under the surface. Bias is rarely obvious because those guilty of it manage to find 'rational' reasons for it, especially when they are unaware that they are guilty of it. To help you avoid bias, I have described in the table on pages 15–16 the main types to which people are subject during appraisal.

## Performance levels

Whether or not your scheme uses performance ratings, it can be useful, when assessing performance, to think along similar lines, which I refer to as performance levels.

The concept is based on the premise that in most situations, some performances will be within the range expected for achievement of the job purpose, some will exceed it, and some will fall short. Performance levels will help you identify what performance fits into which level and, if you determine the appropriate descriptions in advance, it will lessen the likelihood of bias. Let us take our maintenance engineering manager as an example. His performance levels might look like those on page 17:

## *The main types of bias and how to avoid them*

| **Main types of bias** | **Preventive action** |
|---|---|
| ***Horns and halo***<br>Someone does something particularly bad or particularly good and we allow the impression we gained at the time to colour our judgement of them thereafter. It can be particularly subtle because the definitions of good and bad can be very personal to us and actually can have only marginal relevance to performance. | Base appraisal on actual performance against predefined criteria. |
| ***'Recency'***<br>Allowing recent events to outweigh less recent events. As most of us have difficulty remembering what we did two weeks ago, never mind what one of our staff was doing 11 months ago, it is hardly any wonder that recent events carry more weight in our minds than older ones. Yet something that happened 11 months ago should carry the same weight in our assessment as something that happened last week. | Use records of regular informal appraisals rather than rely on memory. |

*continued overleaf*

| Main types of bias | Preventive action |
| --- | --- |

*Sexual and racial discrimination*

A report published by the Institute of Manpower Studies and the Equal Opportunities Commission in 1992 pointed to the potential for appraisers to allow gender stereotyping to influence their assessment of performance. It cited how attributes such as assertiveness were often valued more highly in men than in women and so altered an appraiser's perception of performance. Other sources have pointed towards similar concerns over racial stereotyping, and even a tendency to mark physically attractive people (of either sex) more generously than their less attractive colleagues!

Base appraisal on actual performance against predefined criteria. Question your own values.

*Organisation culture bias*

Bias can vary between organisations. In some organisations, for example technical excellence is prized; in others, it is commitment measured by long hours. Some managers prize initiative while others prize obedience, and some would prefer that every new recruit was a clone of themselves. It is worth considering your own organisation and your personal likes and dislikes. That way, you can begin to identify your own bias tendencies and guard against them.

Base appraisal on actual performance against predefined criteria. Question your own values.

## Performance levels

| | |
|---|---|
| *Significantly exceeds job requirements.* | Achieves all objectives plus develops new procedures and working practices saving considerable sums of money. |
| *Exceeds job requirements.* | Better than expected performance in key areas of response times, staff morale in the face of new working practices and budget control. |
| *Meets job requirements.* | Achieves realistic objectives in key areas. |
| *Does not meet job requirements* | Performance acceptable in most areas but not in any of response times, staff morale or budget control. |
| *Significantly fails to meet job requirements.* | Under-performs in most areas with unacceptable problems in scheduled maintenance, response times, staff morale or budget control. |

Many of these areas could be quantified. Acceptable budget performance could be predefined as $+/- n$ per cent. Performance above a certain level might be very good, while above that level again as outstanding, and so on. Some areas are not easily quantified but can be easily described, such as staff morale in response to the new working practices. We might expect the maintenance engineers to accept the new practices grudgingly, with a short-term effect on response times. If they rebel against them, we might regard that as under-performance by the manager, and if they commence industrial action we might regard that as significant under-performance by the manager. Encouraging the engineers to contribute to the new procedures and actually welcome them, on the other hand, might be seen as significantly above the performance we expected from the manager.

Performance levels work best when descriptions of performance are agreed with appraisees well in advance of their appraisal (say, at the same time that objectives are agreed and at regular reviews thereafter). That way, they know what performance you regard as acceptable, what areas you regard as key, and to what they should devote most attention.

### Performance factors

Understanding the job by looking at its purpose and key result areas, and assessing performance by looking at performance levels, will enable you to accurately assess an appraisee's current performance. This tends to be the most important factor because it is the reason why the job exists, so excellent performance is significant and failure tends to be serious. It can sometimes be easy to assess performance, but it is usually more complex because most people meet job requirements in some areas, exceed them in some, and fall short in others. Appraisers, therefore, have to take into account *all* relevant factors. On pages 19–20 is a list of all the things it is worth considering.

## Performance factors

| Performance factor | Comments |
| --- | --- |
| *Weighting* | Some objectives will be more important than others. Aspects of management relating to development, for example, could be more important than maintenance of the *status quo*. Aspects of a clerical job relating to accuracy might be more important than those relating to standard of dress. Aspects of a production-line job relating to quality might be more important than those relating to interpersonal skills. Different jobs, company cultures and situations require different emphases, be it integrity, creativity, caution or leadership. Long before you begin assessing performance you need to be aware of the relative importance of different aspects of the job requirements, not only so that your assessment can be more accurate but so that you can share that information with the appraisee. |
| *Difficulty* | Satisfactory performance against a tough objective is usually worth more than good performance against a comparatively easy objective. For example, asking a supervisor to implement a new and straightforward procedure will be an easier task than implementing a new procedure which will involve staff in new work rotas and which will require other sections to take on extra responsibilities. |

*continued overleaf*

| Performance factor | Comments |
|---|---|
| *External factors* | External factors can make a given achievement more or less impressive. An information technology manager, for example, who implements a new system within a tight timescale despite a shortage of programmers would probably have performed very well. An order-processing clerk who processed all orders within agreed timescales, despite an unprecedented response to a product promotion, would also have performed very well. |
| *Mitigating circumstances* | Very few of us can totally separate our personal from our professional lives, so problems such as ill health or financial worries can have a detrimental effect on our performance at work. Whether you make allowances for such circumstances in assessing performance, or simply record them as a cause of poor performance, will depend on custom and practice in your organisation. Either way, you should be aware of such problems. |
| *General peformance factors* | Generally we expect people to motivate themselves, to communicate, to work efficiently, to exhibit certain standards of behaviour, dress, time keeping, and so on. We expect them to take decisions and solve problems at their level of accountability. We also expect them to follow procedures but to apply common sense and use initiative where necessary. We also expect energy and commitment. In assessing someone's performance, you will probably need to take account of these general performance factors too. |

## Step 4 – Consider training and development needs

At one time, if someone had a training need the solution was simply to send them on a course. Nowadays, effective managers tend to think of a much wider range of learning experiences.

### Your focus

A helpful focus when considering learning needs is to look at everyday needs and long-term needs:

- Everyday needs concern improving someone's value in their current job, either by rectifying a problem area or by enhancing their skills. The timescale is usually short – days, weeks or months.

- Long-term needs concern improving someone's value to the organisation. The timescale is usually long – months or years.

The common denominator is improving someone's *value*, so let's look at this concept next.

When thinking of increased value, people often cite activities such as working with less supervision, acquiring a distinct competence in something, taking on more responsibility, guiding, developing other staff, leading a project, innovating, widening one's sphere of influence across organisational boundaries, increasing one's influence over larger areas and/or longer timescales, or taking bigger, more complex decisions. There are many naturally-occurring learning opportunities on which you can capitalise. Here are just a few examples:

● Being involved in a project team creates greater knowledge of the subject.

■ Leading a project team provides people-management experience.

▲ Participating in contract negotiations provides legal knowledge, negotiating skills, people skills and understanding of wider issues.

● Teaching other people provides better understanding of the subject matter and people skills.

● Trouble-shooting provides investigative skills and problem-solving skills.

If you add to these learning opportunities the more usual ones of attending courses, evening classes, reading, and other forms of self-study such as videos and audio programmes, you have a good range of alternatives.

**The missing link**. There is one last thing you can do to help develop your staff and that is to *coach*[1] them. Coaching:

● is cheap, easy, enjoyable and satisfying

■ encourages staff to accept responsibility for what they are doing and for the consequences of their actions

▲  improves their ability, adaptability and competence.

Above all, it is the process that makes other learning experiences really work by linking what has been learned to workplace applications.

## Step 5 – Consider the discussion

The discussion is critical to the appraisal process. Not only is it the most visual part of the process, it is the part where emotions can run high, and face-to-face communication skills can be tested to the extreme. If you do not prepare, the discussion can go wrong and detract from the overall process, demotivate the appraisee, upset your working relationship, and undermine your credibility.

There are three critical phases to an appraisal discussion – the opening, the handling of 'tricky bits' and the closing. Let's take each in turn.

### The opening

In any discussion, the opening triggers expectations in the mind of the other person as to what sort of discussion it will be and how it will probably unfold. In this regard, most appraisers are taught to 'put the appraisee at ease' within the first few minutes of the discussion and this is often interpreted as two minutes' idle chat about the weather, this morning's journey into work or the health of the appraisee's family. Every appraisee to whom I have spoken regards this 'relaxing' period as stressful, inappropriate and false. (Having said that, there may be times when it is appropriate. If, for example, the appraisee has had a long journey to reach you, it would be polite to ask about the journey; if you see them infrequently, it would be expected that you bring each other up to date before you begin the appraisal discussion.)

So what should you do? Well, think of it from the appraisee's viewpoint. They want to know the purpose of the discussion, what the outcome will be and how you would like to play it. Knowing the answer to those questions and being involved very early on is the quickest way to relax most appraisees.

There are certain features of an effective opening that are worth emphasising.

- The appraisee is involved within the first few seconds. If you involve them very early, you are signalling that you expect a participative appraisee. I recommend involving them within the first five seconds. For example, 'Thank you for coming along. Have you completed the preparation we discussed?'

- The involvement treats the appraisee respectfully. The questions are valid and easy to answer. For example, 'Would you like me to run through the purpose of the discussion and how I thought we'd go about it?'

- The questions were also useful. There is no point in conducting the discussion as if the appraisee is fully prepared if they have not completed their preparation.

This question, 'Is there anything that has caused you concern that you would like to address early on?' is very useful. There is no point leading the discussion in the order *you* prefer if the appraisee has a burning issue they want to discuss; you will not have their attention until you reach that issue.

● I recommend avoiding the appraiser's 'traditional' opening question, 'So, how do you think things have been going this past year?' This question is so inappropriately broad at this stage of the discussion that it rarely attracts anything other than an extremely guarded 'all right' and, as such, is useless.

### The potentially 'tricky' bits

How do the appraisee's views compare with your own on issues such as overall performance, areas where performance has been better or worse than expectations and the reasons for any variance, mitigating circumstances, strengths and weaknesses, development needs, promotion prospects, and so on? Are there any areas of potential disagreement? If there are, they may well gain amplified importance in the appraisee's mind due to the significance of formal appraisals. So in preparing for the 'tricky' bits, it is worth asking yourself what kind of discussion it will be.

Appraisal discussions have the potential to incorporate other types of discussion. Here is an example. Imagine you are giving an appraisee feedback on under-performance.

Exploring the issue, you discover that the reason for under-performance is one of negative attitude. You may decide the most appropriate action is to shift the discussion into 'disciplinary mode'. If, on the other hand, your exploration reveals a mitigating circumstance relating to a personal problem, you may decide to shift the discussion to 'counselling mode'. Alternatively, the cause of the problem may be a skill deficit, in which case you decide to switch the discussion into 'coaching mode'. During an appraisal discussion, you may shift 'modes' several times depending on the issue under discussion and the most common times to switch modes are the 'tricky' bits. In your preparation, you can help yourself by having a mental dress-rehearsal.

A mental dress-rehearsal is when you harness the visualisation capability of your brain to 'experience' a situation within your mind. You can use it in two ways: to practise your words, and to practise how you will handle 'tricky' bits of the discussion. It can be extremely valuable, because it is virtually as good as a real dress-rehearsal.

It is during 'tricky' bits that you need to pay particular attention to the terminology you use. As anxiety can be a bit high, the scene is set for problems related to *appraisalspeak*!

### What is *appraisalspeak*?
Appraisalspeak is the formal/expected terminology into which we lapse inadvertently during appraisals. It can be written on appraisal forms or spoken face-to-face. The

problem with it is that it detracts from what we are trying to say, it makes us sound inappropriately formal and, in extreme cases, it will even antagonise the appraisee. We can be guilty of it both when writing the appraisal document and face-to-face during the appraisal discussion. Here are some examples, first from appraisal documentation:

- Mr Smith is a valuable asset to the section.

- Miss Jones has made a useful contribution.

- Miss Wise has made a strong contribution to the projects on which she has worked.

- On the whole, Mr Brown has been quite successful.

It would have been better to have written something more descriptive such as:

- Miss Price completed all projects within time and cost budgets. She has been particularly successful in producing results which, for the first time, cast doubt on the safety limits adopted by the customer.

- Mr Jonstone is working in a complex area where there is persistent pressure. Despite this, his quality is consistently high as evidenced by his programming of the AGR project.

- Although Miss Patel encountered some of this work for the first time, she quickly grasped the essentials and produced work that attracted positive reports from the customer.

Here are some examples of face-to-face appraisalspeak:

● **Persistent use of the 'royal we'.** Sometimes this can be a trait specific to the culture of the organisation. It is one favoured by large bureaucracies – and by managers who lack the courage of their own convictions. Its effect is to emphasise the distance between manager and appraisee and to imply that the manager is unsure of his or her ground. Far better to use 'I' when you mean I, reserving 'we' for when you are including the appraisee.

■ **Using 'red rag' words and phrases.** The words 'average' and 'satisfactory' often slip out during appraisal discussions. They might be accurate, but no one likes to be told they are average or satisfactory. As such, these words serve no useful purpose and will probably antagonise the appraisee.

▲ **Inflating the argument.** Telling someone that their performance has been below expected levels can be a bit nerve-racking Some appraisers make themselves feel better by attempting to boost their case. So a 10 per cent shortfall becomes 'A wholly unacceptable performance', an unachieved objective becomes 'thoroughly disappointing', and so on. Again, such terminology serves to antagonise and not persuade.

● **Using parental language**. When parents talk to their children they often do so in an authoritarian manner. 'I would prefer you to do it this way' becomes 'You must do it this way'; 'How would you feel if I suggested...' becomes 'What you ought to do is...'. Suggestions sound like orders and are characterised by imperatives such as 'must', 'ought', 'should' 'can't', and so on. Children do not like being spoken to in this way and adults positively hate it, yet it is a common way for managers to assert their authority. Again, it serves to antagonise.

The rule, therefore, when trying to make your terminology effective is a simple one – be descriptive rather than evaluative in what you say and write.

### The closing

There are two points to note about closing an appraisal discussion effectively. First, whether it has lasted half an hour or half a day, it needs a summary. You will have covered a lot of ground so recap the main points by emphasising what has been agreed and, where actions are required, who is going to do what, and by when. Asking the appraisee to summarise the discussion reveals if your respective recollections differ and so gives you an immediate opportunity to correct any differences. It is also a further way of involving the appraisee in the discussion.

Second, it can be very productive to ask the appraisee how they feel about the discussion, prompting them, if necessary, about any 'tricky' bits. I recommend doing this because if there is a remaining problem it is better to find out about it quickly so that you can pursue it there and then. Also, the fact that you have enquired is a positive stroke for the appraisee which will help your relationship with them.

## Step 6 – Arrange the logistics

It can be surprisingly easy to neglect some of the logistical arrangements you need to make, so here is a list of the minimum that will need your attention.

### Give the appraisee adequate notice

What constitutes 'adequate' will depend on the circumstances, how frequently you have routine appraisals, how complex their situation is, how far ahead they normally book appointments, how far they have to travel to meet you, and so on. A clerk whose performance you review regularly may require only two to three days' notice; a manager whose job involves extensive international travel may require two to three weeks' notice.

### Schedule your own preparation

What preparation do you need to do? Everything contained in this chapter. What information will you need and where will you find it? That depends on the appraisee's job. As a minimum you will probably have to review files and check data and, increasingly, you will have to talk to people to acquire feedback from their internal and external customers, colleagues, other team members, other managers for whom they have completed work, their staff, and so on. This is not 'spying'. It is your genuine attempt to give them quality feedback which is as accurate and complete as possible. The '360-degree appraisal', as it is called, is a growing and worthwhile trend.

There is no short cut to good preparation, so be kind to yourself and fair to the appraisee and schedule it into your diary allowing yourself plenty of time. Finally, remember that one of the benefits of frequent informal appraisals is that your preparation for formal/annual appraisals is a lot quicker and easier than it would otherwise be.

### Identify and book a suitable venue

Appraisals need a private, quiet and preferably neutral venue, such as a meeting room or a vacant office. As a guide, book it (and schedule into your diary) *double* the time you think the discussion will take. That way, if the discussion takes longer you are under no pressure to rush it. Divert telephones and erect a pleasant sign on the door asking that you are not disturbed. Finally, if the choice is your office or the appraisee's, choose theirs; it can be a profitable gesture.

### Have relevant data to hand

Both you and the appraisee want your opinion and comments to be credible and helpful, so be able to refer to relevant data, especially about contentious issues.

## *Self-appraisal questionnaire – preparation*

1 How do you feel about appraisals?

2 To what extent do you use a key result area system (or similar) to understand the jobs you are appraising?

3 To what extent could you be biased in your performance assessments (even inadvertently)?

4 Do you agree detailed performance-level descriptions with staff during the year?

5 Do you use performance-levels as a guide to staff development?

6 To what extent do you identify, use, and communicate to staff additional performance factors?

7 Do you use the concept of added-value to identify development opportunities?

8 To what extent do you use a range of learning experiences to develop your staff?

9 To what extent have you been trained in, and how often do you use, coaching skills?

10 To what extent do you follow these guidelines when preparing for appraisal discussions and arranging logistics?

| | | | | | | |
|---|---|---|---|---|---|---|
| *Don't like them* | 1 | 2 | 3 | 4 | 5 | *Very positive* |
| *Not at all* | 1 | 2 | 3 | 4 | 5 | *All the time* |
| *Too much* | 1 | 2 | 3 | 4 | 5 | *Absolutely never* |
| *Never* | 1 | 2 | 3 | 4 | 5 | *Always* |
| *Never* | 1 | 2 | 3 | 4 | 5 | *Always* |
| *Not at all* | 1 | 2 | 3 | 4 | 5 | *Completely* |
| *Never* | 1 | 2 | 3 | 4 | 5 | *Always* |
| *I don't* | 1 | 2 | 3 | 4 | 5 | *Extensively* |
| *Never* | 1 | 2 | 3 | 4 | 5 | *Constantly* |
| *Not at all* | 1 | 2 | 3 | 4 | 5 | *Totally* |

## Self-appraisal questionnaire

Now please answer the following questionnaire (see page 32–3). By awarding yourself marks out of 5, you can highlight those areas of appraisal preparation in which you will benefit from more attention. The lower the score, the more attention that area needs.

## End-note

[1] See: *The Manager as Coach and Mentor*, Eric Parsloe, London, IPD, 1995.

# the discussion

This chapter is in two parts. In the first part I describe the five characteristics of effective appraisal discussions, and in the second I list the answers to 14 questions that I am typically asked on appraisal. So by the end of the chapter you will have a good and practical grasp of how to conduct the discussion when you are face-to-face with an appraisee.

## Characteristics of an effective appraisal discussion

Here are the five characteristics of an effective appraisal discussion:

### 1 They start on time

Appraisers who are late for an appraisal discussion are sending a clear and discourteous signal to the appraisee about the relative importance of the discussion. Being punctual is your way of saying to the appraisee that both they and the discussion are important.

### 2 The immediate visual impact is positive

You have only one opportunity to make a first impression, so you need to get it right. You should appear to be ready for the appraisal. That means making eye contact with the appraisee, welcoming them in and having a tidy desk that signals 'I am ready and waiting, prepared, and you have my full attention.'

### 3 The discussion is relaxed but businesslike

Good appraisers tend to blend together what mediocre appraisers regard as mutually exclusive, such as a discussion being both relaxed and businesslike.

There are six keys to making an appraisal discussion relaxed but businesslike, some of which were covered in the previous chapter. Where they are repeated, I shall refer to them only as a reminder.

**Get the style right.** On some issues (for example, performance standards or safety) you may have to be immovable but, overall, you and the appraisee are equal parties to the discussion so aim for agreement rather than imposition, and be prepared to compromise on non-critical issues.

**Involve them in the discussion – throughout!** Open-questioning is the easiest and most effective way of involving the appraisee (there is more about this later). You will know if you are on the right lines because the ratio of talking will be well in the appraisee's favour.

**Be open and honest.** It is easy to be less than straight when you fear that what you want to say might upset your working relationship. In my experience, however, the problem is usually in the *way* the message is delivered rather than in the message itself. Again, there will be more on this later.

**Use accurate language rather than *appraisalspeak*.** When describing performance you will speak with more credibility if you are descriptive rather than evaluative and precise rather than vague.

**Stay calm.** Effective appraisals address real issues, and real issues can sometimes be uncomfortable to discuss (especially when they come as a surprise to the appraisee – another reason for regular informal appraisals). A common reaction to criticism, for example, is to counter-attack. So, if you criticise the appraisee, the appraisee counter-attacks, you counter-counter-attack and the conversation is in a downward spiral. Here is an example:

- You were *very* wide of the mark on this objective.

- It was a hellishly difficult objective.

- We've *all* got difficult objectives.

- Yes but we haven't *all* got a key member of staff on long-term sick leave.

- But if you had problems you should have asked me for help.

- If you could only be around more *damned* often I'd have someone to ask.

      – I've got problems too, you know. Have you ever reported directly to a chief executive who treats you as a personal assistant?

The focus of attention in this discussion has moved from the appraisee's under-performance to the appraiser's problems with the chief executive – all because the appraiser did not stay calm and emotionally detached. By remaining detached, the conversation could have gone like this. As you read this version, imagine the appraisee getting more and more heated and the appraiser staying calm. Notice how the appraiser stays detached by acknowledging what the appraisee has said and finding out more relevant information. The temptation to defend or counter-attack is consistently resisted.

      – Achievement on this objective was 25 per cent less than we agreed. Why was that?

      – It was a *hellishly* difficult objective.

      – It was a tough one. You've had tough objectives in the past, however. What was different about this one?

      – For crying out loud, John's on long-term sick leave. *You* know how key he is to this area.

      – When did you know that John's absence would cause a problem with this objective?

      – About half-way through the year.

- Why didn't you come and see me?

- If you could only be around more *damned* often I would have come to see you, wouldn't I? I tried seeing you about it on three separate occasions but you're always running around after the chief executive. You never have time any more.

- I didn't realise I'd become so unavailable. That concerns me. Let's talk about that next. Right now, however, I want to make sure I understand the problems you had with this objective. I need to be clear in my own mind how much was within your control and how much wasn't. Let's begin by looking at the areas in which you needed help.

In this example, the focus has stayed exactly where it needed to stay – on the appraisee's performance. (By the way, if you are thinking that had the appraiser been conducting regular, informal appraisals this issue would never have arisen, you are absolutely correct!)

**Focus on solutions**. Appraisals have a backward-looking element in which you examine past performance, and a forward-looking element in which you decide how the appraisee will do things differently in the future. My recommendation is, when you are examining past performance, to do so with a view to what can be learned from it that will help future performance. This *solution focus* will help appraisees stay open and non-defensive, even when examining 'tricky' bits.

## 4 The discussion sequence is natural

I have heard it said that appraisal discussions should begin on a positive note to relax appraisees and get them 'softened up' for the negative stuff that comes next. Then they should end on a positive note to leave appraisees feeling OK and the appraiser/appraisee working relationship intact. This is, to me, too gross a generalisation. It does, however, contain three elements worth examining.

First, we do want appraisees relaxed quickly so that they will participate openly and freely. I described in the last chapter how to achieve that. Second, we want appraisees in a frame of mind in which they will genuinely receive and consider feedback on their performance and, if they agree, to determine what behaviour changes to make to improve it. I have also described how to do that, and I will have more to say about it in the second part of this chapter. Finally, we want appraisees to leave an appraisal discussion feeling positive about themselves, the appraisal process, and what will happen as a result of it. Achieving these three objectives is more complex than adopting a simple praise/criticism/ praise sequence. It depends on leading the entire appraisal process from start to finish in a positive manner, as described in this book. As for the sequence you adopt for a particular appraisal discussion, I usually make the following recommendation:

- Unless there is anything significantly dominant, follow the sequence of your appraisal documentation. It usually follows a logical sequence – expected performance, actual performance, what the difference tells you about development needs, promotion prospects, and future objectives. This past/present/future sequence is logical enough for formal and informal appraisals. Within each section, I recommend dealing with matters in a sequence that reflects priority. Where an issue is significantly dominant (that is, the appraisee is seriously concerned about an issue such as their job security, lack of promotion, or overall performance-rating) there is little point in talking about anything else until that matter is addressed.

### 5 The appraisee 'owns' the outcome of the discussion

Appraisals are about action as well as record. That action, to be effective, requires the appraisee's commitment, so it is essential that the appraisee 'owns' the outcome of the appraisal. That usually means adopting a style which has the following three characteristics:

- *It is not overprescriptive.* Specify the *what* but encourage them to work out the *how*. There are many occasions when a boss has to specify what will be achieved and that *what* is non-negotiable. Dictating *how* a task should be carried out or an objective achieved, however, is rarely productive. Usually you will get better results if you encourage appraisees to work out how they will achieve what they need to achieve. (Again, I would like to refer you to Eric Parsloe's *The Manager as Coach and Mentor*, London, IPD, 1995.)

■ *Significant issues are given priority, minor issues are not.* The appraisee will more easily generate their performance-improvement suggestions, and more readily accept yours, if you concentrate on the high priority areas. Nit-picking your way through their entire job description, however valid your observations, is contrary to an effective appraisal.

▲ *Manage and monitor the outcome of an appraisal discussion with the same attention to detail as you would for any other business discussion.* Agree with appraisees who will do what, by when, what help will be required, and so on. Determine how you will monitor actions and schedule checks and review sessions in your diary or reminder system. If you demonstrate that you take it seriously, so will your appraisees.

## Questions relating to appraisal discussions

In the second part of this chapter I want to encourage you to tailor the information you receive to your own situation. To help you, I have listed some questions I am typically asked on appraisal skills. That should make it easy for you to focus on areas of concern. (Having said that, you may feel inclined to read them all anyway to broaden and complete your knowledge of appraisal discussions.) The questions are arranged in loose categories relating to face-to-face skills, making feedback productive, and handling common problems. They begin, however, with one that I am always asked on every appraisal skills course.

**1 Is it true that appraisals are more effective if I sit on the same side of the desk as the appraisee?**
The answer to this is yes… and no. Let us deal with the 'yes' first.

Generally speaking, we tend to infer a lot from seating positions. Look at the diagram on page 44 and imagine that it is a rectangular table with six chairs around it, A, B, C, D, E and F. You are seated on chair C. Most people choose chair E for a game of chess or poker and for a disciplinary interview. They would choose chairs B or D for working jointly on a crossword puzzle or resolving a personal problem, and chair A for a selection interview. They make this selection instinctively, signalling that:

- when an interaction is adversarial, very formal, or confrontational we prefer to be directly face-to-face, with a physical object between us

- when an interaction is friendly, non-confrontational, or informal we prefer to be side-by-side or at an angle to one another, not too far apart, with the comfort of a small physical object between us

- when an interaction is as above, but the other person is less well known to us, we retain the angled positioning

*Seating positions*

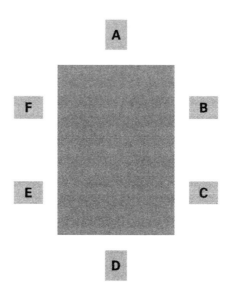

but feel more comfortable with increased distance between us.

Consequently, we infer from a seating arrangement what kind of interaction it will be; formal, informal, confrontational, friendly, and so on. Hence the received wisdom about not putting a 'barrier' between you and the appraisee.

My preference is to hold appraisal discussions in the neutral territory of a meeting room and to work across the corner of the desk or table. That way I am signalling that the discussion is an informal, 'joint' activity, yet we have the comfort of a small physical object between us which is also a convenient writing surface.

Now for the 'no'. If you spend all year speaking to your staff across your desk without any problems and for the annual appraisal discussion you waddle your chair to their side of the desk, you will look like someone who has just read a simplistic book on appraisal and your gesture will be received with the contempt it deserves. What you can do, however, is to put the visitor's chair across the corner of your desk rather than on the opposite side of the desk, and make that its normal position. (If you have insufficient room for this layout your office is probably too small for the 'status' desk position of facing the door; turn it to face the wall and you will also reap the benefit of easier concentration when working alone.)

## 2 Should I keep on my knee the notes I write so that the appraisee cannot read them upside down?

No, keep them on the desk in full view so that the appraisee can read them easily upside down! Appraisals are most effective when they are open between the two of you. Even if what you are writing is totally benign, if the appraisee cannot see it suspicions may arise. You should not be writing anything that you would not say to the appraisee face-to-face. Furthermore, to maintain your attention on what the appraisee is saying, keep any notes brief. Use key words that you can expand on later. If you need to write down something verbatim, explain what you are doing and ask the appraisee to pause while you do so.

**3 Is it true that we should ask open questions rather than closed ones?**

As a very general rule, open questions are more productive than closed ones. To say that open questions are good and closed questions are bad is like saying that hammers are useful and screwdrivers are not. They are simply different tools for different jobs.

Closed questions are good for checking facts and understanding.

- 'Have you done the preparation we discussed?'

- 'So, to summarise, what you are saying is… Is that correct?'

Open questions, on the other hand, are good for exploring issues, feelings, etc.

- 'How did you find the preparation?'

- 'What other areas have caused you concern?'

- 'If I suggested… how would you feel?'

You will have noticed that responses to closed questions are usually brief ('yes') although sometimes people will expand voluntarily ('Yes, I did the preparation last week. It was quite revealing. What really struck me was…'). Responses to open questions, on the other hand, are usually more elaborate, providing opportunities for you to probe deeper by asking further related open questions 'Really, in what way?', 'What else did you try in response to that obstacle?'

Closed questions, because we have the option of a brief response, are easier to answer but the involvement of the appraisee is less. Open questions generate more information, more dialogue, and more involvement and so will help create more 'ownership' of the discussion. So the bottom line is to use both closed and open questions, but to get the best out of the discussion use many more open than closed questions. (You will find more on questioning in Ian MacKay's *Asking Questions*, London, IPD, 1995.)

### 4 How do I not only listen but show that I am listening?

The problem for most of us is that people speak much more slowly than our brains think so we get ahead of them in the conversation. Listening requires a still mind, a genuine desire to understand – and three powerful techniques.

**Look as if you are listening**. Get your posture and position right. Sit reasonably upright and lean back slightly. Adopt an asymmetrical posture (that is, be different either side of an imaginary dotted line drawn down your middle by, say, crossing your legs or leaning on one elbow). Point your torso and feet slightly away from the other person but point your head towards them and look at them. Get your facial expression right. Most of the time your facial expression needs to be neutrally pleasant no matter what you are thinking inside. Finally, get your eye contact right; 50 to 70

per cent is enough to show you are listening and to pick up
the visual clues of body language from the other person that
are all part of the communication process.

**Ask relevant questions**. Probe deeper into what you are
hearing. As a broad guideline, probe for at least three
questions beyond the initial question before you move on to
another topic. For example:

- Why was this project three weeks overdue?

- I needed help on it and you were abroad.

- What sort of help did you need?

- I needed information from the marketing department
  and they were too busy. So I needed someone to speak
  to the marketing manager. I felt as if I couldn't because
  I'm too junior.

- In what way did you feel too junior?

- Well... she's always very busy and seems to fob me
  off.

- What alternatives did you consider?

- Well... none, really. I just waited for you to return.

- What would you like to do differently if the same
  situation arose again?

**Prove you are listening**. The easiest way to prove you are listening is to repeat back what the other person has said to you. There are two ways to do this, both very useful. The first is reflecting. That is when you repeat the phrase the other person has just said. You can reflect when they have said something and stopped, and you want them to continue telling you more:

- ... I felt as if I couldn't because I'm too junior.

- You felt too junior.

- Yes, more senior people seem so much more assertive. I just can't argue against them.

That is useful information; it has clarified what the appraisee meant by 'too junior'.

The second way to prove you are listening is to summarise. If the other person has said so much you want to pull together the various things they have told you, or if you want to punctuate one section of the discussion and move on to the next, or if they are just rambling and you want to get them back on track, summaries are useful. (There is more on this topic in Ian MacKay's *Listening Skills*, London, IPD, 1995.)

### 5 If I let the appraisee talk too much, won't I lose control of the discussion?

Not if you remember this: it is easy to think and listen at the same time but not so easy to think and talk at the same time.

Consequently, the person who asks the questions tends to be in control of the pace and direction of the conversation, not the person doing the talking.

## 6 What should I do if the appraisee is too quiet, too talkative, over-emotional or manipulative?

First, let us try to understand why people behave in these ways:

- People can be too quiet because they are naturally shy, because they believe their role in appraisal is to sit and listen, or they want to say something very important but are unsure how to phrase it.

- Shyness can also make people too talkative. By filling the space with chatter, they shut out serious issues that feel threatening.

- People can be over-emotional because they feel stressed or threatened. Their defence mechanism is to go on the attack or become very defensive and their response appears over-emotional.

- People can be manipulative because their repertoire of face-to-face skills is extremely limited, and manipulation is the only option they feel they can use.

Whatever it is they are doing it is in your interests to avoid labelling them quiet, garrulous, emotional or manipulative. It is their behaviour that is causing the problem so that is what you have to address. By adopting the right behaviours yourself you may be able to trigger the desired behaviour from them.

So for the quiet person, begin the discussion in 'safe' areas to get them used to participating, then gently probe their answers. Try paraphrasing the question until you get an answer, then probe on it. Also, be alert for the person who suddenly goes quiet when you broach a particular topic. That usually signals that you have touched a nerve, so paraphrase your question using more gentle language.

Closed questions are very useful for interrupting talkative people. When they answer, you can probe their response to get them back on the point. You can even ask them directly, 'How does that relate to the subject we are discussing?'

When someone appears over-emotional they either have, or feel they have, a valid reason to be upset, so you need to find out what their concerns are. The best way is to acknowledge their concern and begin probing.

The first thing to do with manipulative behaviour is to recognise it. Sometimes it can be obvious, such as shouting, using dominant body language, or being sarcastic. Sometimes it can be subtle, with a spurious logic. Imagine talking to an appraisee about promotion prospects in a 'flatter' organisation. You try explaining that regular and routine steps up the ladder are now a thing of the past but that other, albeit less predictable, opportunities are likely to arise, to which they respond, 'Well that's no good. How can I plan my future on that basis? Would you like to be in a position where you can't tell how long you'll be in this grade? Would you like to be told you're ready for promotion but that there are no vacancies? Would you?' The obvious answer is 'Of course not', but that is what they want to hear. It is also completely beside the point because the structural shift most organisations in Western economies are experiencing these days are well outside the appraiser's control. What the appraisee is attempting to do is to trigger your emotions, making you feel uncomfortable so that you will concede the point just to avoid the discomfort. If you can recognise the attempted manipulation you can keep the discussion truly solution-oriented, acknowledging it and then returning it with a question. For example, 'I can see you're concerned about this. Let's look at it in detail. Do you see this as something that is happening in our organisation alone or in others too?' Delivered in a neutral tone of voice, showing that you are not rising to the bait, this response is also good for shouting, physical domination, and sarcasm.

### 7 How can I respond to an appraisee who is concerned that they are not being promoted?

It depends on the reason. There are two main ones. First, they could be good enough to be promoted but there is no suitable vacancy for them. The best response is to be honest. Empathise with them but focus strongly on the fact that there has to be a suitable vacancy. Also explain what you are doing, what you will continue to do, and what they can do, to locate such a post.

Second, they may not be ready for promotion. It is a common misunderstanding that just because someone is performing well that promotion is theirs by right. In such situations, I recommend that you remind them that promotion is not a reward for good performance in one's current post; the route to promotion is to demonstrate the competencies required in the larger post. That is not as 'catch 22' as it sounds because it is possible, and useful, to develop someone's abilities in whatever post they are in. Leading a project team, for example, will provide people-management experience without actually having any staff.

The *way* you point this out, however, is important. An adversarial approach will be totally counter-productive. Questions such as these, asked genuinely with a neutral tone of voice, will help the appraisee work out the situation for themselves: 'What do you know about the criteria for promotion?'; 'How do you compare against those criteria?'; 'What have you done yourself to gain the required competencies?'; 'I'd like to help. Let's look at what we can do to get you into a strong position. Which skills do you feel you need most?'

Finally, there is one point in which I believe passionately – your staff are an organisational resource, not your personal resource. To deny someone an opportunity of promotion because of the problems their promotion might cause you is unforgivable, and a rapid route to appraisee demotivation and under-performance.

## 8 How do I handle someone who disagrees with the overall performance rating?

I have two parts to this answer. The first may seem unhelpful but is genuinely meant. It is this – do not get yourself into that position in the first place. The problem is usually of the appraiser's making. It is almost always avoided when you and the appraisee have agreed well in advance the job purpose, key result areas, performance levels and other performance factors. Do that and hold regular informal appraisals, and appraisees virtually identify their own overall performance rating. On the rare occasions when they do not (and this is the second part of the answer) all you have to do is refer to the performance levels and ask *them* to justify the rating they feel is appropriate (rather than *you* justify the rating you feel is appropriate).

## 9 What should I do when the appraisee disagrees with my rating and persistently tries to make comparisons with other members of staff?

Agreeing performance levels, combined with regular informal appraisals, nips most such problems in the bud. Where, nevertheless, you find yourself in this situation all you can do is state that you will not discuss their performance with any other member of staff and so you will not discuss the performance of any other member of staff with them. This is their appraisal and so it is on their performance that you will focus. This answer, however, creates distance between you both which needs to be minimised with empathy, listening, body language, and involvement through probing. As with question 8, it is better not to be in that position in the first place. Regular, informal appraisals help to keep you out of such predicaments.

**10 How can I motivate someone at the top of their pay scale/near retirement/who cannot be promoted due to lack of opportunity?**

The question is a regular one in organisations where people were once accustomed to annual increments and regular promotions but who are now faced with a 'flatter' structure and leaner times. Their 'mind-set' lags behind the new reality and they feel let down by the new situation.

When the question is asked, I cannot help but notice that appraisers feel that the problem is theirs and they should have an answer to it, and they feel guilty that they do not. In answer to the question, therefore, I make a general point first. Appraisees are being paid for what they contribute to organisational performance, not for their attendance. They have no right to throttle back just because they have reached the top of their pay scale, are nearing retirement, or cannot find a suitable vacancy for promotion.

Another point I make is that when people feel deprived it is because they are comparing themselves against something. So, rather than feel guilty because you do not have a magic wand, encourage them to see their situation more realistically.

That takes us to the third part of my answer. If we want to alter someone's expectations so that they are based more in the current reality rather than a past reality, the first thing we need to do is show empathy. You can do this by acknowledging their feelings and comments. Try reflecting back what they have said to demonstrate that you have heard it, paraphrase it so that you show you understand it, and ask relevant questions to demonstrate your genuine interest.

The best way to encourage them to view their situation differently is to resist the temptation of talking at them, and to ask questions that will prompt their thoughts. ('How have criteria for promotion changed recently?'; 'If you are at the top of your pay scale, does that mean you are being paid above or below average for the job?'; 'If you only have eighteen months to go before you retire, do you want to look back on this period as a waste of your life or would you prefer to look back on it with satisfaction?') These questions are just examples; you will need to string together several questions, probing more deeply as you receive answers. You may not conclude the issue in one discussion. At the first attempt you may just sow the seeds of new thoughts, cultivating them in subsequent discussions. Throughout, however, your aim is to encourage your demotivated appraisee to see the situation differently, not to rely on you to wave a magic wand and make their problem go away.

Finally, in answer to this question, I remind people that anyone who is close to retirement, or who is at the top of their pay scale, or who is capable of promotion but cannot find a vacancy, probably has a wealth of experience. Recognising that experience and harnessing it in specialist work, project leadership, training less experienced personnel, or representing their section to other areas or outside bodies, can provide a significant motivational boost. Such activities can also provide just the skill development, job experience and exposure to more senior decision-makers that these people seek.

### 11 How do I give praise without making it sound false or 'sugary'?

Effective praise is a powerful motivator. Yet it is something we tend to do too infrequently and too ineffectively. You can praise at any time, and appraisal discussions are a natural opportunity – but watch for these typical faults:

- We praise too unspecifically. A general 'well done' is meaningless if the recipient does not know what we are referring to.

- We praise too frequently which devalues the currency.

- We praise superficially. Praising while giving out attention elsewhere such as reading a file, as a by-the-way remark while talking about another topic, shows that we do not care about the praise.

- We praise conditionally. That is, we give praise at the same time that we ask for something, such as a favour, acceptance of a delegated task, agreement to work late, and so on. As a result the praise is seen as a 'softening-up' process or a precondition.

● We contaminate praise by mixing in a bit of criticism. ('That was a great presentation. I wish your written work was as good').

The steps to effective praising are really quite straightforward.

**Be specific**. Describe what it is you are praising. Was it the way the appraisee used their initiative? Was it the way they worked through lunch for a week to get the job completed within the deadline set by the customer? Was it the way they have persevered with further education, studying during evenings and weekends to improve their prospects?

**Give positive strokes**. That is, do something which makes them feel good. For example, describing how you feel about what they have done (pleased, proud, excited, etc), making eye contact with them and asking questions to understand better what they did, what decisions they took, etc, will all let them appreciate that your praise is genuine.

**Seek to expand the behaviour**. This point is relevant to all but minor praiseworthy actions, and is especially relevant to praising during appraisal discussions. Ask questions to help the appraisee determine what they learned, how they can do it even better next time and in what other situations they can apply what they have learned. That way the praising becomes a mini-coaching session.

These steps will ensure that your praising stays positive and effective.

## 12 How do I criticise without making it sound like a reprimand?

Let us begin by looking at why criticism is so often a problem:

● Some people are too liberal with their criticism. For them, there are two ways of tackling any job – their way and the wrong way.

■ We tend to have subconscious memories of being criticised as children. The feelings associated with those memories (anger, guilt, injustice) are 'replayed' when we are criticised in adult life. Consequently, we react negatively to criticism.

▲ Knowing that an appraisee may well react negatively to criticism, however justified, can trigger appraisers' 'fight or flight' response. With the former, they tend to go in too hard, exaggerating the point, and with the latter they tend to sugar-coat or dilute the point; its effect is minimised.

So, here are the steps to constructive criticism:

**Criticise in private**. It is more considerate of the appraisee, and hence you are more likely to have a productive discussion.

**Criticism is most effective when it is timely**; that is, when it happens quickly after the event. So you need to act quickly, as long as emotions are not running too high, and not save up critical points for appraisal discussions. Nothing in an appraisal discussion should come as a surprise. That way, when you raise critical issues during appraisals, you are summarising previous conversations, not presenting issues for the first time.

**Use specific and descriptive terminology** rather than personal, emotional, judgemental or evaluative terminology. Be concise.

**Check with the appraisee that your description is correct**, even if you are 100 per cent sure of your facts. This allows for the occasions when you are not in possession of all the facts and have, effectively, got it wrong; second, it lets the appraisee see that you are being fair.

**Describe the behaviour you want to see in the future**. Behaviour does not exist in a vacuum, so if you want the appraisee to cease certain behaviour you have to replace it with something else.

**Remind the appraisee that the problem is the behaviour, not them as a person**. Your intention, remember, is to modify their behaviour. You will stand a better chance of achieving this goal if they feel OK about both the process and about themselves. The rule is – be tough on behaviour but support the person.

13 How can I phrase criticism so that it does not cause offence?

Focusing on the behaviour rather than the person, and being specific and descriptive, will enable you to avoid most problems. There may be occasions, however, when some 'fine tuning' is required. These occasions will be when the criticism and/or the source of the information is sensitive and, to maintain the appraisee's attention on the need to modify behaviour, you want to choose your words carefully. Here is an example.

Imagine that your appraisee is a team leader and that you have been approached by several members of his team voicing concern about his frustrating and annoying attention to unnecessary detail at the expense of overall productivity. What they say fits your impression of the team leader and you decide to raise it with him. You could open the conversation by saying, 'It has been brought to my attention that you pay too much attention to detail and not enough to overall productivity', which sounds both horribly formal, and as if you have spies watching his every move. Alternatively, you could grab the bull by the horns; 'You're paying too much attention to detail at the expense of overall productivity', which is making an unsubstantiated accusation. On the other hand, you could be accurate in your description of what you know to be true and you could involve him at the same time: 'Are you aware that your staff have the impression that you pay more attention to unnecessary detail than you do to overall productivity?' You are still tackling the issue directly but you are broaching the subject in a descriptive manner. You are also recognising the very real issue that, even if the staff are incorrect in their assumption, they still have that impression and they are reacting accordingly. This phraseology can also have the effect of shifting focus slightly from the fault of the appraisee to the impression of his staff and how they might have gained that impression. It is slightly less personally judgemental, and hence the appraisee may be less defensive and more open than might otherwise have been the case.

### 14 How can I set really meaningful objectives?

Let us begin by examining the problem. In the last decade, jobs have become more output-oriented so more people are working with objectives. When discussing objectives with people, I see how easy it is to fall into common objective-setting traps. As you read them, ask how many apply to you.

**Being imprecise** to the extent that there could be considerable debate about the achievement of the objective, how to monitor it or even what it means. Here are some real examples: 'Maintain expertise in fluid dynamics and deploy to customer benefit in all circumstances'; 'Contribute to the effectiveness of the team'; 'Attend safety meetings'; 'Ensure that staff are developed to their full potential'. At the end of the review period, there could be considerable debate about whether or not they have been achieved. The usual response is only to write objectives that can be quantified, but then some people...

**...quantify the wrong things**. It is a well-established rule in management that what gets measured gets done but it applies *literally*, so if an appraiser quantifies the wrong things, the wrong things will be achieved. Requiring someone to increase customer contact by 25 per cent may not result in more sales, just more customer contact. Specifying increased productivity may result in lower overall output if quality is ignored, so increasing reject-rates. There can also be unforeseen repercussions. Requiring senior police officers to improve figures for crime detection per officer may result in higher crime rates if officers are taken away from crime *prevention* to improve the crime *detection* figures. Consultant clinicians can achieve targets for shorter waiting lists by accepting fewer new patients for treatment. Crazy though these examples may sound, they are both true!

**Ignoring some key result areas** because they 'cannot be quantified'. Key result areas such as image, morale, teamwork, development of staff potential, and so on are very difficult to quantify without complex surveys, so rather than write imprecise objectives appraisers ignore them altogether. My advice in such circumstances is to accurately describe the performance we want without actually quantifying anything. For example, 'improve staff morale from a situation where productivity is low, short-term absenteeism is high, and staff are applying for numerous vacancies at the same grade, to one where these three indicators are reversed'; or 'ensure that all staff have a personal development plan that will improve their long-term value to the company and which will remove "lack of development" as a reason cited for resignation'. That way, performance can still be monitored and measured.

**Writing objectives that relate only to the formal appraisal period**. Most formal appraisal periods are annual and so some appraisers assume that objectives have to cover a 12-month period, no more and no less. Yet their 'real life' job objectives may cover periods of, say, three to 18 months. Being unable to reconcile this dilemma, they write appraisal objectives which get salted away with the appraisal documentation and have little relevance to the job. They then write job objectives as and when they are required. Understandably, appraisees pay attention to the job objectives and ignore the appraisal objectives. My advice is to write and appraise on job objectives.

The best way to avoid these objective-setting pitfalls is first, to treat objectives as a dynamic management and personal development tool, relating them to the job, reviewing them regularly, and monitoring progress closely. Second, to make your objectives SMART. I have come across several SMART mnemonics related to objectives. This, I think, is the best one:

**Specific and Stretching**. Objectives have to be clear and concise and relate to one issue only. They should also be a bit beyond the appraisee's ability so that they will learn and develop as a result of the challenge.

**Measurable**. If they are measurable, you will avoid factual disagreements and subjective assessments; you will also find it easier to monitor progress. 'Measurable' does not just mean time and cost; descriptive objectives can also be measurable.

**Achievable, Agreed, Accepted**. Unachievable objectives demotivate, and so do objectives that are forced on the job holder. Objectives agreed, or at least accepted, as a result of dialogue usually work.

**Relevant**. The degree to which they are achieved should impact directly on fulfilment of the job purpose. If there is no impact, the objective is probably irrelevant. Using the key result areas system described in Chapter 2 helps to ensure that objectives are always relevant.

**Trackable**. If the job-holder's progress cannot be monitored, it is a poorly written objective and should be reworded. This last element, trackable, is important enough to warrant special mention. Trackable objectives provide the opportunity to obtain warning of deviations, 'fine tune' performance, and coach for further development. If objectives are not trackable, not only is it impossible to monitor progress, but vital opportunities for routine appraisal discussions are being missed.

## *Self-appraisal questionnaire – the discussion*

1 To what extent do you recognise how much responsibility you have for the effectiveness of appraisal discussions?

2 Do your appraisal discussions start on time?

3 Is the immediate visual impression of the discussion venue positive?

4 To what extent are your appraisal discussions relaxed but businesslike?

5 Do your appraisal discussions follow an effective sequence?

6 To what extent do your appraisees 'own' the outcome of their appraisal discussions?

7 Does your use of open questions need improving?

8. Would your appraisees describe you as a good listener?

9 How well do you maintain control of the discussion without dominating it?

10 How would you describe your handling of quiet, talkative, emotional, and manipulative appraisees?

11 How well do you handle the 'tricky' bits of appraisal discussions?

12 To what extent do you write SMART objectives?

| | | | | | | |
|---|---|---|---|---|---|---|
| *I don't* | *1* | *2* | *3* | *4* | *5* | *Totally* |
| *Rarely* | *1* | *2* | *3* | *4* | *5* | *Always* |
| *Rarely* | *1* | *2* | *3* | *4* | *5* | *Consistently* |
| *Rarely* | *1* | *2* | *3* | *4* | *5* | *Fully* |
| *Sometimes* | *1* | *2* | *3* | *4* | *5* | *Tailored to each appraisee* |
| *Sometimes* | *1* | *2* | *3* | *4* | *5* | *Always* |
| *Yes* | *1* | *2* | *3* | *4* | *5* | *Not at all* |
| *Probably not* | *1* | *2* | *3* | *4* | *5* | *Consistently* |
| *Not very well* | *1* | *2* | *3* | *4* | *5* | *Very well* |
| *In need of improvement* | *1* | *2* | *3* | *4* | *5* | *Very effective* |
| *Not very well* | *1* | *2* | *3* | *4* | *5* | *Very effectively* |
| *I don't* | *1* | *2* | *3* | *4* | *5* | *Totally* |

# conclusion – making time for appraisal

If, as I hope, you can see the benefits of making regular appraisal part of your management style, you may be wondering where you could find the extra time. So, here are six suggestions which participants on appraisal programmes have told me have proved particularly useful:

● Review the performance of each member of staff every month and ask them to produce a summary of the discussion (one handwritten side of A4, maximum). They keep the original, you keep a copy. Even if you only complete nine or ten such reviews a year, preparation for annual appraisal is consistent between you and your appraisees, it takes less time and is better quality.

■ Do the same type of review and file-note every time something significant happens, both good and bad. Again, ask the appraisee to write the file note (you can correct it if necessary). Disagreements over appraisal ratings are reduced dramatically because you are both working from the same information.

▲ Apply a car-service analogy to appraisals. You do not give your car a full service every weekend – you check safety items such as oil, water, and tyres. Every few thousand miles, you have the oil and filters changed during an intermediate service. The car has a full service at longer intervals, perhaps annually, and, at even longer intervals, it has a major service. If you think of the annual appraisal as the full service, every couple of years you might have to go into more detail (the major service) as you discuss career prospects, but monthly appraisals are the equivalent of routine safety checks, with an intermediate appraisal every three to six months, depending on the appraisee's needs.

To continue the analogy a little further, if you think you do not have time for proper appraisals, you are probably thinking like the car driver who does not have time to stop for petrol – sooner or later you will have to so you might as well plan for it.

- Change the style of discussions you already have so that they become appraisal discussions. If you meet a member of staff once a month to check the progress on project x, make it an appraisal discussion about the progress on project x.

- Agree performance-level descriptions with each member of staff, identify where performance needs improving, and agree development/coaching plans to improve performance in each area. Not only does this reduce disagreements during annual appraisals, it enables you to put leadership principles and coaching skills into practice.

● Use self-monitoring of performance wherever possible so that appraisees 'own' the performance data. This makes the data more credible. It also means that they may know of, and correct, their performance problems before you do. That way, they can tell you about their successes rather than listen to you telling them about their failures.

As I mentioned earlier, whatever the range of appraisal systems you experience, there will be one constant – the effectiveness of the appraisal discussion can determine the effectiveness of the whole appraisal system, your working relationship with the appraisee and your credibility as a boss. That is why it is so important to make the appraisal discussion positive and productive because the process you go through to make it effective is sound management practice – and that is in everyone's interest.

# further reading

BLANCHARD K. and SPENCER J. *The One Minute Manager*. London, Fontana, 1983.

FLETCHER C. *Appraisal – Routes to improved performance*. 2nd edn. London, IPD, 1997.

GILLEN T. *Assertiveness for Managers*. Aldershot, Gower, 1992.

GILLEN T. *Positive Influencing Skills*. London, IPD, 1995.

HONEY P. *Improve Your People Skills*. 2nd edn. London, IPD, 1997.

HONEY P. *101 Ways to Develop Your People Without Really Trying*. Maidenhead, Peter Honey, 1994.

MACKAY I. *Asking Questions*. London, IPD, 1995.

MACKAY I. *Listening Skills*. London, IPD, 1995.

PARSLOE E. *The Manager as Coach and Mentor*. London, IPD, 1995.

PEASE A. *Body Language*. London, Sheldon Press, 1981.

Other titles in the *Management Shapers* series:

## Asking Questions

Ian MacKay

*Asking Questions* will help you ask the 'right' questions, using the correct form to elicit a useful response. All managers need to hone their questioning skills, whether interviewing, appraising or simply exchanging ideas. This book offers guidance and helpful advice on:

● using various forms of open questions – including probing, simple interrogative, opinion-seeking, hypothetical, extension and precision etc.

■ encouraging and drawing out speakers through supportive statements and interjections

▲ establishing specific facts through closed or 'direct' approaches

● avoiding counter-productive questions

● using questions in a training context.

Second Edition
96 pages
Pbk
0 85292 768 1
November 1998
£5.95

## Assertiveness

Terry Gillen

*Assertiveness* will help you feel naturally confident, enjoy the respect of others and easily establish productive working relationships, even with 'awkward' people. It covers:

- understanding why you behave as you do and, when that behaviour is counter-productive, knowing what to do about it

- understanding other people better

- keeping your emotions under control

- preventing others bullying, flattering or manipulating you against your will

- acquiring easy-to-learn techniques that you can use immediately

- developing your personal assertiveness strategy.

First Edition
96 pages
Pbk
0 85292 769 X
November 1998
£5.95

## Constructive Feedback

Roland and Frances Bee

*Constructive Feedback* plays a vital role in enhancing performance and relationships. The authors help you identify when to give feedback, how best to give it, and how to receive and use feedback yourself. They offer sound, practical advice on:

- distinguishing between 'destructive' criticism and 'constructive' feedback

- using feedback to manage better – as an essential element of coaching, counselling, training and motivating your team

- improving your skills by following the 10 Tools of Giving Constructive Feedback

- dealing with challenging situations and people

- eliciting the right feedback to highlight your strengths and opportunities for your own development.

First Edition
96 pages
Pbk
0 85292 752 5
1998
£5.95

**The Disciplinary Interview**

Alan Fowler

*The Disciplinary Interview* will ensure you adopt the correct procedures, conduct productive interviews and manage the outcome with confidence. It offers step-by-step guidance on the whole process, including:

- understanding the legal implications

- investigating the facts

- presenting the management case

- probing the employee's case

- diffusing conflict through skilful listening and questioning

- distinguishing between conduct and competence

- weighing up the alternatives – dismissing or dropping the case; disciplining and improving performance through counselling and training.

First Edition
96 pages
Pbk
0 85292 753 3
1998
£5.95

## Leadership Skills

John Adair

*Leadership Skills* will give you confidence, guide and inspire you on your journey from being an effective manager to becoming a leader of excellence. Acknowledged as a world authority on leadership, Adair offers stimulating insights on:

- recognising and developing your leadership qualities

- acquiring the personal authority to give positive direction and the flexibility to embrace change

- acting on the key interacting needs – to achieve your task, build your team and develop its members

- transforming the core leadership functions such as planning, communicating and motivating, into practical skills you can master.

First Edition
96 pages
Pbk
0 85292 764 9
November 1998
£5.95

## Listening Skills

Ian MacKay

*Listening Skills* describes techniques and activities to improve your ability and makes clear why effective listening is such a crucial management skill – and yet so often overlooked or neglected. Clear explanations will help you:

● recognise the inhibitors to listening

■ improve your physical attention so you are seen to be listening

▲ listen to what is really being said by analysing and evaluating the message

● ask the right questions so you understand what is not being said

● interpret tone of voice and non-verbal signals.

Second Edition
96 pages
Pbk
0 85292 754 1
1998
£5.95

## Making Meetings Work

Patrick Forsyth

*Making Meeting Work* will maximise your time – both before and during meetings – clarify your aims, improve your own and others' performance and make the whole process rewarding and productive – never frustrating and futile. The book is full of practical tips and advice on:

- drawing up objectives and setting realistic agendas

- deciding the who, where and when to meet

- ▲ chairing effectively – encouraging discussion, creativity and sound decision-making

- sharpening your skills of observation, listening and questioning to get across your points

- dealing with problem participants

- handling the follow-up – turning decisions into action.

First Edition
96 pages
Pbk
0 85292 765 7
November 1998
£5.95

## Motivating People

Iain Maitland

*Motivating People* will help you maximise individual and team skills to achieve personal, departmental and, above all, organisational goals. It provides practical insights on:

- becoming a better leader and co-ordinating winning teams

- identifying, setting and communicating achievable targets

- empowering others through simple job improvement techniques

- encouraging self-development, defining training needs and providing helpful assessment

- ensuring pay and workplace conditions make a positive contribution to satisfaction and commitment.

First Edition
96 pages
Pbk
0 85292 766 5
November 1998
£5.95

## Negotiating, Persuading and Influencing

Alan Fowler

*Negotiating, Persuading and Influencing* will help you develop the critical skills you need to manage your staff effectively, bargain successfully with colleagues or deal tactfully with superiors – thus ensuring that a constructive negotiation process leads to a favourable outcome. Sound advice and practical guidance is given on:

- recognising and using sources of influence

- probing and questioning techniques to discover the other person's viewpoint

- adopting collaborative or problem-solving approaches

- timing your tactics and using adjournments

- conceding and compromising to find common ground

- resisting manipulative ploys

- securing and implementing agreement.

First Edition
96 pages
Pbk
0 85292 755 X
1998
£5.95

## The Selection Interview

Penny Hackett

*The Selection Interview* will ensure you choose better people – more efficiently. It provides step-by-step guidance on techniques and procedures from the initial decision to recruit through to the critical final choice. Helpful advice is included on:

- drawing up job descriptions, employee specifications and assessment plans

- setting up the interview

- using different interview strategies and styles

- improving your questioning and listening skills

- evaluating the evidence to reach the best decision.

First Edition
96 pages
Pbk
0 85292 756 8
1998
£5.95

## Working in Teams

Alison Hardingham

*Working in Teams* looks at teamworking from the inside. It will give you invaluable insights into how you can make a more positive and effective contribution – as team member or team leader – to ensure your team works together and achieves together. Clear and practical guidelines are given on:

● understanding the nature and make-up of teams

■ finding out if your team is on track

▲ overcoming the most common teamworking problems

● recognising your own strengths and weaknesses as a team member

● giving teams the tools, techniques and organisational support they need.

First Edition
96 pages
Pbk
0 85292 767 3
November 1998
£5.95